A Donation has been made to the
Clay County Public Library
In Memory Of:

Richard Roberts

This Donation has been made by:

Roger & Pat Roberts

Discovering Giganotosaurus

Written by Rena Korb
Illustrated by Ted Dawson

Content Consultant:
Kenneth Carpenter
Curator of Lower Vertebrate Paleontology & Chief Preparator
Denver Museum of Nature and Science

visit us at www.abdopublishing.com

Published by Magic Wagon, a division of the ABDO Publishing Group, 8000 West 78th Street, Edina, Minnesota 55439.

Printed in the United States.

Text by Rena Korb
Illustrations by Ted Dawson
Edited by Jill Sherman
Interior layout and design by Emily Love
Cover design by Emily Love

Library of Congress Cataloging-in-Publication Data
Korb, Rena B.
  Discovering Giganotosaurus / Rena Korb ; illustrated by Ted Dawson ; content consultant, Kenneth Carpenter.
    p. cm. — (Dinosaur digs)
  ISBN 978-1-60270-106-9
  1. Giganotosaurus—Juvenile literature. I. Dawson, Ted, 1966- ill. II. Title.
QE862.S3K67 2008
567.912--dc22
                        2007034050

FOSSIL FINDS

Ruben Carolini enjoyed hunting fossils in the badlands of Argentina, South America. In 1993, he spotted a gigantic bone. He called two professors, Rodolfo Coria and Leonardo Salgado, to tell them of his find.

The scientists thought Carolini had found a bone of a plant eater, or herbivore dinosaur, since many had been found in the area. When they saw it, they realized the fossil was from a carnivore—and one that was bigger than *Tyrannosaurus rex*.

The scientists dug up the bones and spent two years studying them. In 1995, they shared their findings with the world. They had discovered one of the largest meat-eating dinosaurs to walk on Earth. They named it *Giganotosaurus* (jee-guh-NOH-toh-sor-uhs).

Since then, scientists have found fossils belonging to other giant meat eaters in Argentina and Africa. As of 2007, *Mapusaurus*, *Spinosaurus*, *Carcharodontosaurus*, and *Giganotosaurus* all compete for the title, "king of the carnivores."

Hong was only nine years old, but he knew a lot about dinosaurs. Hong had just received a postcard with a special message for him. The postcard had only one word written on it.

Hong smiled. Hong and his father, a paleontologist, had helped on a dig not too long ago. They helped scientists uncover a new species of dinosaur. The message was from the scientists who were studying their find. This meant that the scientists had finally named the dinosaur. The message read, "GIGANOTOSAURUS."

Hong stared at the message. He remembered that dig well. It was one of the most exciting digs he had ever been on!

Months earlier, Hong had heard his father talking about a new discovery. A team of paleontologists had uncovered a gigantic new species of dinosaur in South America. They had invited Hong's father to join their dig. Hong wanted to go, too.

Hong stood outside the study waiting for his parents' decision. With fingers crossed, he watched the door swing open. One look at his father's face gave Hong his answer. He was heading to South America!

Giganotosaurus lived about 95 million years ago in Argentina.

On the plane ride, Hong's father told him that a fossil hunter had been searching in the dry, windy badlands of Argentina. He noticed a huge bone poking out from a hill. He called some scientists to come see it.

"Many fossils of plant eaters have been found in the area," Hong's father explained. "So that's what the scientists thought they would dig up. But after the bone was free, they saw it was thin and hollow. The bone was layered like an onion and fanned out in a crest on one end."

"That means it was the bone of a carnivore," Hong said. "Meat-eating dinosaurs had layered, thin bones. The crest means it was a shin bone. Shin bones on carnivores fanned out near the knee."

Giganotosaurus could track and kill dinosaurs that were much larger and heavier than itself. It may have even snacked on *Argentinosaurus*, which was almost twice its size!

By the time they reached the dig, Hong was ready for work. He was not tired, even though they had traveled thousands of miles.

The scientists welcomed Hong and his father. They started to describe the discovery. They had uncovered the thigh bone. It measured four feet eight inches (1.4 m) long.

At first, Hong could not speak. What he had just heard seemed impossible. "That means . . . that means that the dinosaur was a carnivore that was bigger than *Tyrannosaurus rex*!"

New Dinosaur   Tyrannosaurus Rex

- Weighed about 8 tons
- up to 48 ft long (14.6m)
- hands with 3 fingers
- Carnivore with teeth that sliced thru flesh
- Lived about 95 million years ago
- Lived in South America

- Weighed about 6 tons
- up to 45 ft. long (13.7m)
- hands with 2 fingers
- Carnivore with teeth that crushed flesh & bone
- Lived about 65 million years ago
- Lived in North America

Hong could not help speaking up. "Are we going to see the dinosaur now?" he asked.

The adults laughed. "It's too late tonight, Hong," explained his father. "But the bones have been there for millions of years. They'll still be there in the morning."

Hong fell asleep almost as soon as his head hit his pillow. He dreamed of dinosaurs.

Giganotosaurus weighed more than eight tons (7 t). That is how much 290 second graders would weigh if there was a scale big enough to hold them all!

The next day, Hong was ready before the sun came up. The team led Hong and his father across the bare, brown land, weaving around short, yellow shrubs. These were the only plants that grew on the badlands.

Suddenly, a gigantic fossil was before them. The bones of its spine stretched out like a thick, long snake. The skull was the size of a bear. The thigh bone was bigger than Hong.

The skull of *Giganotosaurus* was six feet (2 m) long. When scientists compared it to fossils of other meat eaters, they found that *Giganotosaurus* may have been related to a dinosaur that lived in Africa.

The team had been digging for several days.

"Once we're done, we can figure out the mysteries locked in the fossils," one of the scientists explained to Hong. "How big was the dinosaur? How much did it weigh? When did it live? We have guesses, but we want answers."

"We're lucky to be part of this discovery," Hong's father said. "Have you got your tools, Hong? We have digging to do!"

Hong and his father worked on one part of the skull, which had broken into several pieces. With a dental tool and an awl, Hong carefully dug the soft rock away from the jawbone and the teeth that were still attached to it.

Then, Hong used his small brush to remove the stubborn dirt. He carefully touched the long, sharp teeth. They were also serrated, like the edge of a saw. They easily would have sliced through the flesh of any animal the dinosaur chose for dinner.

When he was done, Hong got out his notebook. In this notebook, he wrote down notes about all the fossils he found on digs. He opened to a new page and carefully drew a picture of the jawbone and teeth.

He also pulled out his tape measure to see just how long those teeth were. Hong recorded the number in his notebook: ten inches (25 cm).

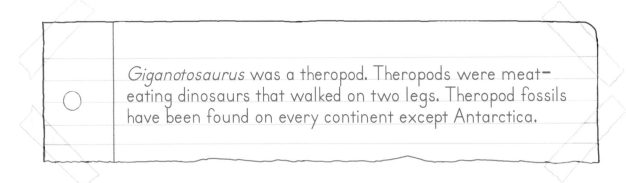

Giganotosaurus was a theropod. Theropods were meat-eating dinosaurs that walked on two legs. Theropod fossils have been found on every continent except Antarctica.

Only then did Hong stop to see the team's progress. He and his father joined the other scientists gazing down at the huge skull that was still half-buried in the dirt.

"The dinosaur's brain was held in this part of the skull," Hong's father said.

Hong looked at the opening. It was the size of a softball. The dinosaur's body was huge, but the brain was small. Hong knew this meant the dinosaur was probably not as smart as others, such as *T. rex*.

Many record-holding dinosaurs once lived in South America. The continent was home to some of the oldest dinosaurs, as well as some of the biggest and heaviest dinosaurs.

Over the next few days, the team dug up more bones. By the time they were done, the dinosaur lay in a pit 20 feet (6 m) deep, 30 feet (9 m) wide, and 30 feet (9 m) long!

To study the fossils, the scientists had to move them from the dinosaur's resting place to a laboratory. They soaked strips of burlap in plaster and water. They wrapped one side of each bone with the burlap. When it was dry, they flipped it over to cover the other side. To Hong, it looked like wrapping a birthday present.

Scientists discover a new kind of dinosaur about every six weeks. When this happens, they study the fossils of similar dinosaurs. This helps them figure out what the new dinosaur was like.

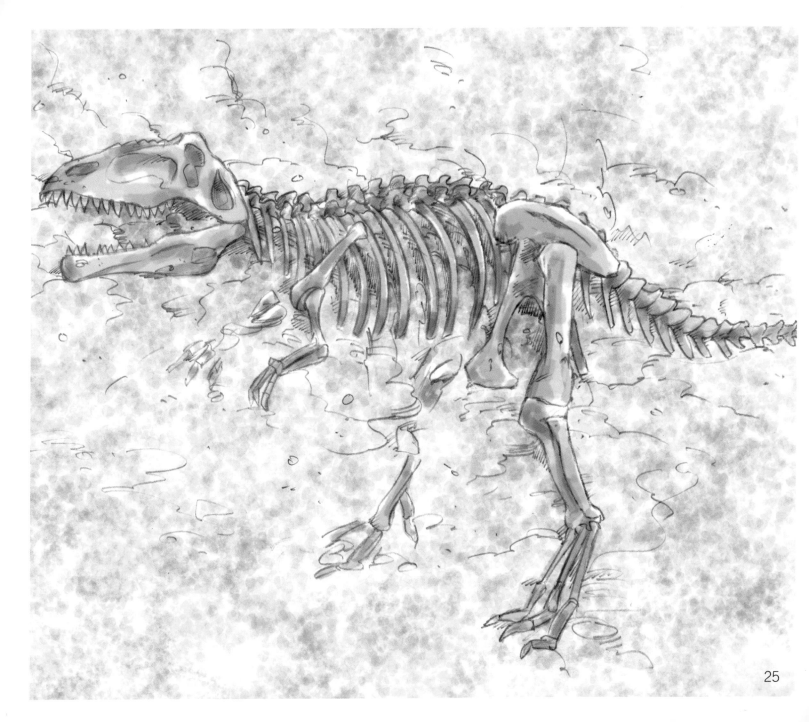

Finally, the team was ready to load the bones on the trucks. The paleontologists would return to their laboratory to work on the fossils. Hong and his father would make the long journey home.

As they said good-bye, the paleontologists told Hong about the work ahead of them. They had to clean the bones and put them back together. They had to study the bones to learn their secrets. Scientists often spend years studying the dinosaur bones they find. They share what they have learned by writing articles for scientific magazines.

The team also needed to name their dinosaur.

"We'll let you know what it is," said one of the paleontologists. "But by then, you'll probably have forgotten about our friend here."

Hong shook his head. No matter how many digs he went on, he would never forget this one!

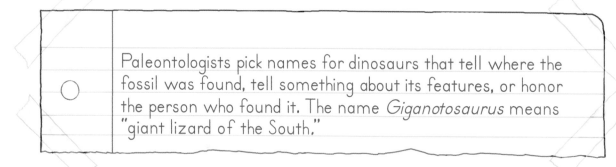

Paleontologists pick names for dinosaurs that tell where the fossil was found, tell something about its features, or honor the person who found it. The name *Giganotosaurus* means "giant lizard of the South."

ACTIVITY: Tools for Digging

What does a paleontologist use these tools for?

1. small brushes

2. notebook

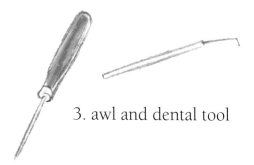

3. awl and dental tool

4. plaster and burlap strips

ANSWERS:
1. to remove loose dirt from bones; 2. to write down notes about fossils; 3. to scrape away dirt from bones; 4. to wrap up bones for moving

GLOSSARY

awl — a tool with a sharp point.

badlands — a region where plant life is scarce and where natural forces have worn away the soft rocks into sharp and complicated shapes, such as peaks and gullies.

carnivore — an animal that eats flesh.

dig — a place where scientists try to recover buried objects by digging.

fossil — the remains of an animal or a plant from a past age, such as a skeleton or a footprint, that has been preserved in the earth or a rock.

paleontologist — (pay-lee-ahn-TAH-luh-jist) a person who studies fossils and ancient animals and plants.

serrated — with small V-shaped teeth along the edge, like a saw.

species — a class of animals of the same kind and with the same name.

READING LIST

Currie, Philip J., and Colleayn O. Mastin. *The Newest and Coolest Dinosaurs.* British Columbia, Canada: Grasshopper Books, 1998.

Dalla Vecchia, Fabio Marco. *Giganotosaurus.* Detroit: Blackbirch Press, 2007.

Dixon, Dougal. *Dougal Dixon's Amazing Dinosaurs.* Honesdale, PA: Boyds Mill Press, 2000.

Lessem, Don. *Bigger than T. Rex.* New York: Crown Publishers, 1997.

ON THE WEB

To learn more about *Giganotosaurus*, visit ABDO Publishing Company on the World Wide Web at **www.abdopublishing.com**. Web sites about *Giganotosaurus* are featured on our Book Links page. These links are routinely monitored and updated to provide the most current information available.